This storybook is an extension of The Mussel Hatchery exhibition which opened at Philadelphia's Fairmount Water Works on February 17, 2017.

www.mightymussel.com

A combined living science laboratory and interactive exhibition, the Mussel Hatchery reveals the secret power of these small bivalves to improve our environment significantly. Our water experts, including the Philadelphia Water Department (PWD), leading the nation in citywide stormwater management; the Partnership for the Delaware Estuary (PDE), champion of aquatic restoration; and the Academy of Natural Sciences of Drexel University, which pioneered research on aquatic diversity and pollution, are hard at work caring for mussel babies, conducting water quality tests and contributing to current research within the Mussel Hatchery Lab. The science lab is truly a living exhibit that constantly improves with new research and innovation. The goal: advance hatchery techniques and develop protocols to support future mussel production and wide-scale use of mussels to improve the health of the watershed. PDE has received $7,934,000 in funding from the Pennsylvania Infrastructure Investment Authority (PENNVEST) to construct a freshwater mussel hatchery that will produce hundreds of thousands of mussels annually, which is likely to serve as a scalable model, nationally and globally, for nature-based solutions to the health of freshwater systems.

The Mussel Hatchery has been supported by The Pew Center for Arts & Heritage with additional support from the Philadelphia Water Department, The McLean Contributionship and PA Department of Natural Resources and Conservation.

Victoria Prizzia, Founder and President of Habithèque Inc., served as creative lead and project director of the Mussel Hatchery Exhibition from concept to fruition. Habithèque works as a cultural producer, creating informal educational exhibitions, events and digital resources to fulfill a critical need: educating the public about nature-based solutions to some of the planet's most critical challenges. Victoria's body of work brings together artists and scientists to demonstrate how we can build a more just and sustainable future for all living things. She creates cleverly whimsical cultural experiences in museums and public spaces that connect individuals to their own curiosity and creativity. She uses beauty as a threshold to prepare individuals to be more open to challenging ideas and complex or unfamiliar stories. Victoria believes that change happens through progressive ideas, creative innovations, and emotional connections that build lifelong enthusiasm and empathy for the natural world. Her exhibitions work to build an informed and engaged citizenry by connecting the act of play and discovery with real world challenges and personal choices.

www.habitheque.com

THIS BOOK BELONGS TO:

....

To Ava P and all of the small and mighty characters of our world, sharing their magic here, there and everywhere.

Special thanks to Karen Young, Joanne Dahme, Craig Barron, Stacy Levy, Kurt Cheng, Dr. Danielle Kreeger and Angela Padeletti.

THE FLOWING RIVER...

Where finned, furred, shelled, feathered and the invisible swim, hop, flutter, float and crawl in an ever-changing watery world.

The river can whoosh, whirl and roar.

It can also be very still.

She's waiting not just for **ANY** fish but a *particular kind* of fish for her *particular kind* of babies.

Lucky for momma, the river water flows.

It means that things come to her, which is necessary because she rarely wanders in this ever-dynamic world.

She has the wisdom to know...

And **THOUSANDS** of her *precious babies* enter the water.

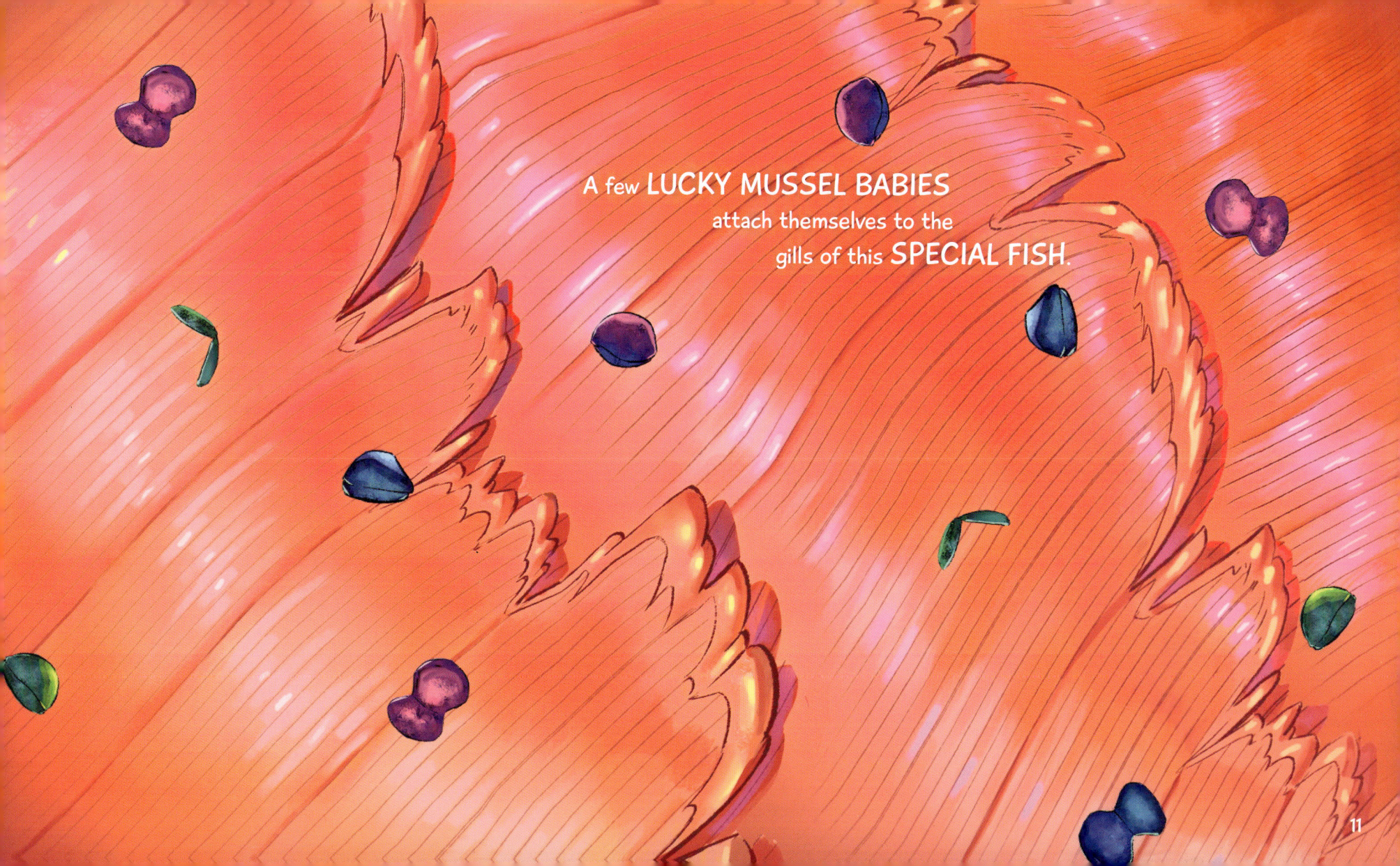

Momma's newborn adventurers are hitching a ride!

Whoosh!
 Gurgle!
  Flow! "Ciao, Ciao Momma!"

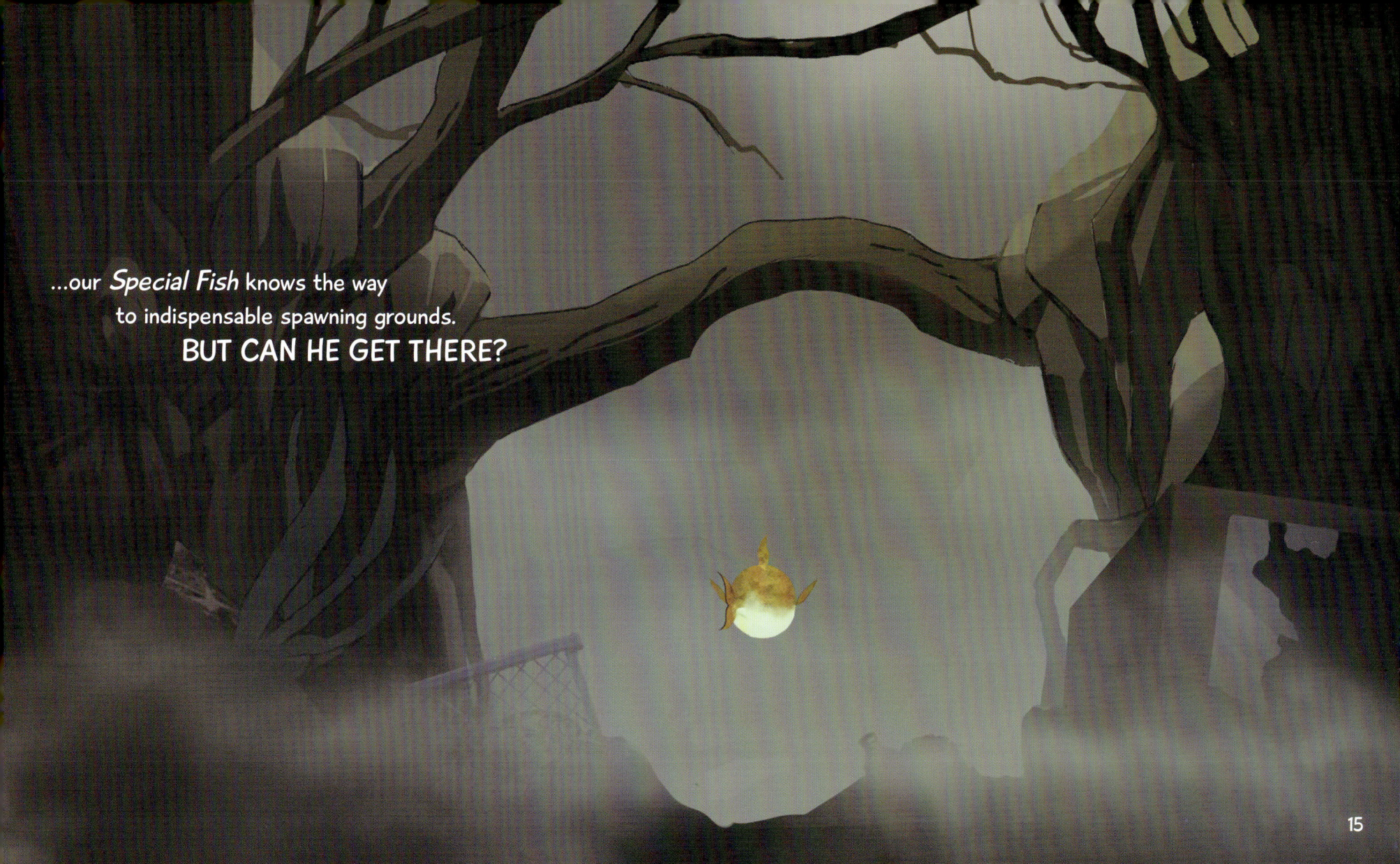

...and man-made structures such as dams that   PREVENT FISH MOVEMENT UP-STREAM!

...all hurt our rivers, streams and the magnificent characters who swim, hop, flutter, float and crawl there.

Traveling many weeks together, our mussels are now **BIG ENOUGH** to make it **ON THEIR OWN** in the wild.

Babies no more, these adolescent mussels, now with their own hard shells, drop off of the Special Fish to nestle into the floor of the river.

"Thank you Special Fish!"

"What a ride!"

This riverbed is home. For some mussels, life could last for **MORE THAN 100 YEARS.**

And that is *good news for the river* because these mighty characters improve their river environment and our world **JUST BY BEING ALIVE.**

Eating and breathing, mussels siphon solids from the water, as
BREAKFAST, LUNCH, DINNER and **AFTERNOON TEA!**

Shwoop!

Slurp!

Ahhh.

DE • TRI • TUS
DETRITUS

"Yum, yum!"

Mussels filter water to live.

PHY · TO · PLANK · TON
PHYTOPLANKTON

"Crunch, crunch!"

They suck in water, trapping pollutants and other solids.

"Munch, munch!"

They use some of the food to grow.

ZO·O·PLANK·TON
ZOOPLANKTON

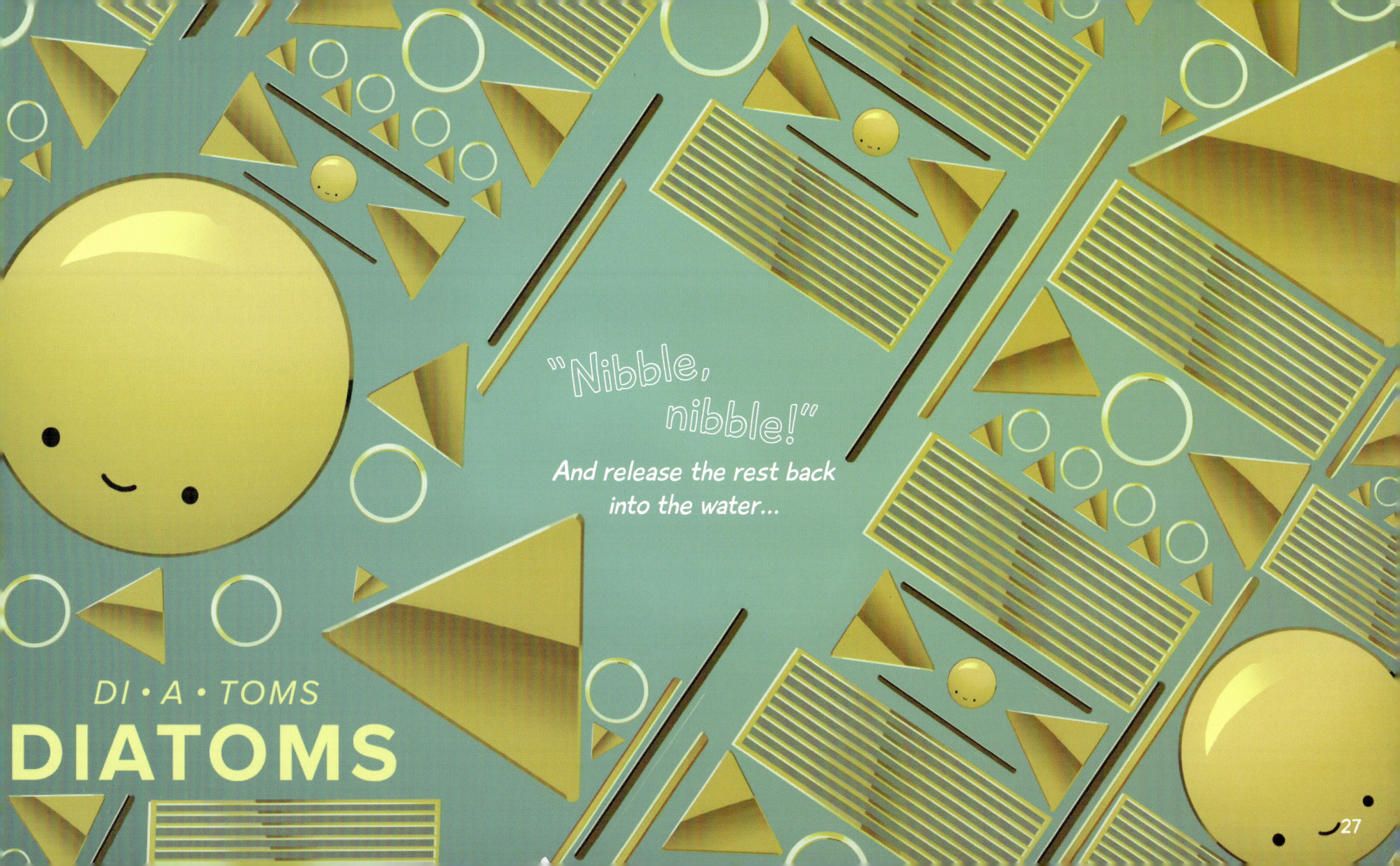

A single mussel can clean up to 20 GALLONS of water EACH DAY! Think of what a HUNDRED or even a THOUSAND MUSSELS can filter!

"Can I have some more please?"

Our mussel population has now grown from a few to many mussels. **THOUSANDS OF MUSSELS.**

This riverbed is our dream realized.

Glossary

PAGE	WORD	DEFINITION
6	Ever-dynamic	Always changing
15	Spawning	Giving birth to a large number of eggs into water
16	Pollution	Making the world around us dirty or harmful to our health
22	Environment	The surroundings in which a person, animal or plant lives
23	Siphon	Some water animals, like clams or mussels have a siphon, which is a special part of their body, a tube they use to suck in food and water and push out waste.
24	Detritus	Bits of left-over stuff. Yucky to us, but good for mussels to eat.
25	Phytoplankton	Extremely tiny plants that live in water and you need a microscope to see
26	Zooplankton	Very tiny animals that live in water and eat phytoplankton
27	Diatoms	A one-cell plant that lives in water and has a very hard cell wall—as hard as a shell
28	Bacterium	A one-cell form of life: different kinds live everywhere on earth and in our bodies. Some are helpful to us, some make us sick.
30	Imperiled	Put at risk of being harmed, injured or destroyed
32	Habitat	The natural home or environment of an animal, plant
32	Diversity	Showing a great deal of variety

Read-Aloud Tips
Children who love to read do better in school.

YOU are the best person to support your child's reading ability. You have advantages you may not realize:

- You can SNUGGLE while you read together. When you add love and warmth to reading, you are building a lifelong love of books.
- You KNOW YOUR CHILD BEST. You don't need to read the whole book in one sitting. You can skip the parts they don't like, or just look at the pictures together.
- You can CREATE READING TRADITIONS that are special to your family. Bedtime is great, but so is early morning or while waiting for appointments.

Reading, talking, rhyming and playing and even "getting into things" are valuable learning experiences for children. Children love to repeat things: reading the book again, or doing the activities again feeds their brain development. They become the experts.

WHEN YOU READ TOGETHER, YOU LEARN TOGETHER.

These self-guided tips and activities were developed to strengthen the role of caregivers and older siblings as primary influencers in growing literacy skills in everyday life. With support from the William Penn Foundation, Fairmount Water Works leads a community-based partnership program called The Watershed is an Open Book, *to build literacy skills for families and young children.*

Karen Lefkovitz, Early Childhood Literacy Specialist, is an educational consultant who specializes in early literacy and family learning, with a focus on informal education.

Ellen Freedman Schultz, Director of Education Partnerships at the Fairmount Water Works, develops and manages environmental education programs related to water quality, watershed management, and the history of Philadelphia's municipal water system.